For Sandie, with love - R.E.
For the Cherrys, with love - C.F.

OXFORD
UNIVERSITY PRESS

Great Clarendon Street, Oxford OX2 6DP

Oxford University Press is a department of the University of Oxford.
It furthers the University's objective of excellence in research, scholarship,
and education by publishing worldwide in

Oxford New York

Auckland Bangkok Buenos Aires Cape Town Chennai
Dar es Salaam Delhi Hong Kong Istanbul Karachi Kolkata
Kuala Lumpur Madrid Melbourne Mexico City Mumbai Nairobi
São Paulo Shanghai Singapore Taipei Tokyo Toronto

Oxford is a registered trade mark of Oxford University Press
in the UK and in certain other countries

British Library Cataloguing in Publication Data available

ISBN 0-19-910886-2 Hardback
ISBN 0-19-910887-0 Paperback

3 5 7 9 10 8 6 4 2

Printed in Hong Kong

Nonsense
Christmas
Rhymes

Poems by Richard Edwards

Illustrated by Chris Fisher

OXFORD

UNIVERSITY PRESS

While Shepherds Watch

While shepherds watch their flocks by night
They sometimes fall asleep,
That's one of the big dangers when
Your job is counting sheep.

Last Christmas

Last Christmas,
While feeling quite jolly,
I pulled on a cracker and, golly!
A froggy jumped out,
Went leaping about,
And hopped off to hide
in the holly.

The Holly and the Ivy

The holly and the ivy –
One's prickly, one's not,
I sat down on the prickly one
And in the air I shot,

And shot up through the ceiling,
And shot up in the sky,
And wished a 'Merry Christmas' to
The pigeons passing by.

I shot above the rainbow,
And climbing towards heaven,
I wished a 'Merry Christmas' to
A Boeing 747.

I kept shooting higher
And higher, and soon
I was wishing 'Merry Christmas' to
The man in the moon.

Then I started to tumble
To fall back to earth,
To slow me down, I flapped my arms
For all that I was worth.

I fell back through the ceiling
And landed on a chair,
But luckily on a different one,
And the holly was not there.

So just you be careful
When Christmas comes round –
Be sure to check beneath you when
You're starting to sit down.

And just you remember
The thing I forgot:
The holly and the ivy –
One's prickly, one's not.

Little Robin Redbreast

Little Robin Redbreast
Sat upon a tree,
'Chirrup, chirp,' and 'twitter,'
And 'tweet-tweet-tweet,' went he,
And 'caw,' and 'screech,' and 'gobble,'
And 'cock-a-doodle-doo,'
And 'oink,' and 'miaow,' and 'ee-aw,'
And 'baa,' and 'grunt,' and 'moo,'
And 'grr!' and 'bzzz,' and 'ribbit,'
And 'bow-wow-wow,' went he,
As Little Robin Redbreast
Sat upon a tree.

Thank You Very Much

Last Christmas you gave me
Some weeds and a nettle,
The Christmas before that
A rusty old kettle,
The Christmas before that
A bottle of fog,
The Christmas before that
Three hairs from your dog,
This Christmas you gave me
Some mud from the ground,
So what will I get
When next Christmas comes round?

Silent Night

Silent night? No, not quite!
Crackers bang like dynamite,
In the living room Uncle Sam's snores
Shake the windows and rattle the doors,

Oh, for some heavenly peace!
Give me some heavenly peace!

Silent night? No, not quite!
Turn the telly down! Kids, don't fight!
Hi-fi's blaring, and what's that roar?
Gran's decided to vacuum the floor,

Oh, for some heavenly peace!
Give me some heavenly peace!

Silent night? No, not quite!
Joe, don't pinch! Dawn, don't bite!
And don't try climbing the Christmas tree…
Crash! Please, somebody rescue me!

Oh, for some heavenly peace!
Give me some heavenly peace!

Look! It's Snowing

Look! It's snowing cornflakes
And wheaty biks as well,
And honey nutty hoops, and look!
Some choco pops just fell,
And frosted rings and puffy rice,
So fetch a bowl and spoon,
I'll bring the milk and sugar
And we'll eat all afternoon!

Christmas is Coming

Christmas is coming,
The geese are getting fat,
So they're going to the health club
To make their tummies flat,
They're lifting weights, they're jogging,
They're rowing on machines –
And all so they can squeeze into
Their tight blue jeans.

A Purple Christmas

I'm dreaming of a purple Christmas
With purple all around,
With purple snowmen made of purple snow
On purple ground,
With purple Santa pulling on
The purple suit he'll wear,
And purple reindeer galloping
Up through the purple air,
And purple Christmas dinner
With purple things to eat –
Purple roast potatoes
And purple turkey meat,
And purple decorations
On a big, bright purple tree,
And presents wrapped in purple paper –
All for purple me!

Good King Wenceslas

Good King Wenceslas looked out,
Snow was falling quickly,
'Got to get the shopping in,'
Said the King, 'and quickly.'
Jumped on to his mountain bike
Turned the pedals faster,
Skidded on a patch of ice,
Ended up in plaster.

Poor Father Christmas

Poor Father Christmas,
He had to go to bed,
His throat was sore, his nose was blocked,
His eyes were watery red.
'Whatever shall I do?' he sighed,
'I've got to do my rounds,
But oh, my aching joints! And how
My poor head pounds!'

'You're not going anywhere,'
Santa's wife replied.
'I can take your place tonight
While you stay warm inside.
Rudolph knows the way to go,
And I can drive the sleigh,
So you sip your hot lemon, love,
And I'll be on my way.'

She harnessed up the reindeer,
She checked the sacks were full,
She put on Santa's suit and made
A beard from cotton wool,
Then off she sped into the sky,
And no-one ever knew
That Mother Christmas called that year
When Father had the flu.

The Flying Christmas Pud

Lulu had a brainwave –
She'd make a Christmas pud,
A Christmas pud so tasty,
The best pud that she could.

But when she tried to cut it,
It took off with a zoom,
And circled round the kitchen
And flew out of the room.

Christmas pud! Christmas pud!
Stop that Christmas pud!
Lulu wants to eat it,
It looks so blooming good.
Oh, Christmas pud! Christmas pud!
Flying on the breeze,
Lulu wants her pudding back,
Stop that pudding, please!

Lulu chased her pudding
Outside into the street,
A policeman tried to catch it,
It knocked him off his feet.

It circled round the town hall
And headed out of town,
Across the fields and forest
And up the hills and down.

The last time it was spotted
It was flying out to sea,
A ship's captain reported it
Beside the Zuider Zee.

Christmas pud! Christmas pud!
Stop that Christmas pud!
Lulu wants to eat it,
It looks so blooming good.
Oh, Christmas pud! Christmas pud!
Flying on the breeze,
Lulu wants her pudding back,
Stop that pudding, please!

A Letter from Santa

Dear deer,

Thank you,
Thank you for your work,
You were great on Christmas Eve,
You never tried to shirk,
I never heard one grumble,
You're faithful, fast and strong,
You never slip or stumble
As you haul the sleigh along.
What would I do without you?
So, thank you once again,
And I hope you are enjoying
Your holiday in Spain –
Trotting through the warm sea,
Soaking up the sun,
Dancer, Vixen, Donner,
Comet, everyone,
Dasher, Blitzen, Cupid,
Prancer, Rudolph too –
Bring me back a souvenir,
A sunny day would do!
That's all, I'll have to stop now,
I'm needed in the stores.

Hugs and kisses, love you lots,
Your best friend,

Santa Claus X

All I Want for Christmas

All I want for Christmas is a mammoth,
A mammoth, just a mammoth,
All I want for Christmas is a mammoth –
All shaggy with a great big roar.

All I want for Christmas is a mammoth,
A mammoth, just a mammoth,
All I want for Christmas is a mammoth
To chase away the dog next door.

All I want for Christmas is a mammoth,
A mammoth, just a mammoth,
All I want for Christmas is a mammoth
To hoover round the kitchen floor.

All I want for Christmas is a mammoth,
A mammoth, just a mammoth,
But if the pet-shop doesn't have a mammoth,
I'll be happy with a dinosaur!

Auntie Mimi's Mistletoe

Auntie Mimi's mistletoe –
She ties it to her head,
And goes round kissing everyone,
She's kissed my Uncle Fred,
She's kissed my Mum, she's kissed my Dad,
The postman and the cat,
She kissed the man next door so hard
She squashed his glasses flat,
She's kissed my little brother,
Though he hid behind the tree,
And now she's coming my way
But she won't get me!

The 26th of December

The day after Christmas,
And out in the yard
Two snowmen in shorts are fighting hard,
And why are they fighting?
That's easy to say,
The day after Christmas is Boxing Day.

In the Bleak Mid-Winter

In the bleak mid-winter
   Wrap yourself up tight,
Put on extra undies,
   Extra socks at night,
Extra fleecy jumpers,
   Extra gloves and scarves,
Make yourself some ear-muffs
   Out of grapefruit halves.

In the bleak mid-winter
   Don't forget your knees,
Wind them round with tin-foil
   To keep out the breeze.
Spread a layer of mustard
   Underneath your vest,
Tie hot-water bottles
   Tightly to your chest.

In the bleak mid-winter,
   Knit yourself a hat,
Knit one for your neighbour,
   Knit one for the cat,
Put on baggy trousers,
   Stuff their legs with hay,
In the bleak mid-winter
   Keep the frost away!

Carole Carroll

When Carole Carroll's carol-singing
Carole Carroll's carols,
Carole's carols sound so bad
That people hid in barrels,
Yes, people run and block their ears
And hide away in barrels,
When Carole Carroll's carol-singing
Carole Carroll's carols.

I Saw Three Drips

I saw three drips come leaking in
  On Christmas day, On Christmas day,
I caught them in a biscuit tin
  On Christmas day in the morning.

The drips became a steady pour
  On Christmas day, on Christmas day,
That washed me through the kitchen door
  On Christmas day in the morning.

I floated on the muddy tide
  On Christmas day, on Christmas day,
A whale came bobbing by my side
  On Christmas day in the morning.

The whale came home for toast and tea
  On Christmas day, on Christmas day,
We sang songs round the Christmas tree
  On Christmas day in the morning.

This Christmas

This Christmas I won't buy a tree,
I'll stretch my arms instead,
And stand up in the window
With a fairy on my head,
With tinsel wrapped all round me
From my shoulders to my toes,
And presents piled up to my knees,
And glitter on my nose.

Christmas at the Zoo

Early Christmas morning,
Christmas at the zoo,
They've all hung up their stockings –
The gorilla and the gnu,
The walrus and the crocodile,
The skunk, the kangaroo.

Let's see what Santa's brought them
To unwrap on Christmas Day –
For the chest beating gorilla
There's a bongo drum to play,
For the gnu a box of gnougat,
For the skunk, deodorant spray.

A rattle for the bushbaby,
Playing cards for the cheetah,
Belgian chocolate covered ants
For the greedy anteater,
Some scissors for the walrus
To keep his moustache neater.

Balloons for the baboons,
Toothpicks for the crocs,
Ribbons for the gibbons,
Skis for the Arctic fox,
For the octopus in the aquarium
Four pairs of woolly socks.

There's a joke book for the hyena –
Hyenas love to laugh –
A jumper for the kangaroo,
And as for the giraffe –
A very, very, very, very,
Very long scarf.

There's eye-shadow for the panda,
A brush for the mountain hare,
Sticky sweets for parakeets,
A teddy for the bear,
And for the bald-headed eagle,
A nice warm hat to wear.

Yes, early Christmas morning,
Christmas at the zoo,
They're so pleased with their presents
The gorilla, the gnu,
The walrus and the crocodile,
The skunk, the kangaroo.